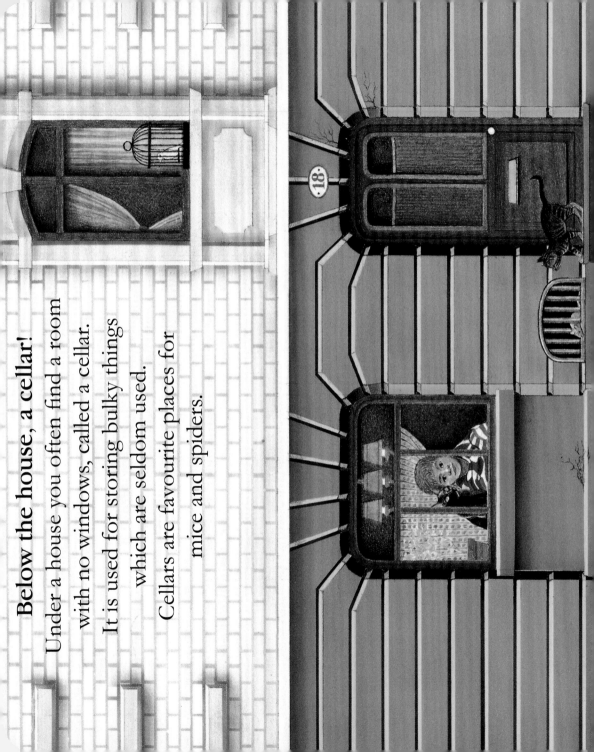

Below the house, a cellar!

Under a house you often find a room
with no windows, called a cellar.
It is used for storing bulky things
which are seldom used.

Cellars are favourite places for
mice and spiders.

Life Below the City

Illustrated by Ute Fuhr and Raoul Sautai
Created by Gallimard Jeunesse and Claude Delafosse

MY FIRST DISCOVERY PAPERBACKS

Below the city it's dark. You can't see anything, but there's lots going on!

In this book you can see everything down below, like on a guided tour.

Thanks to a simple torch made of paper, you can explore the dark pages of this book. It's like magic!

You'll find the torch on the last page.
Press it out and slide it between
the plastic pages and the black pages.

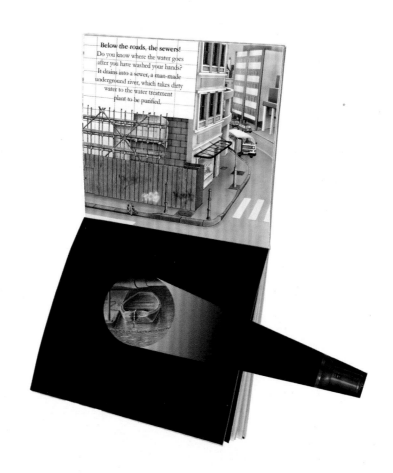

As you move it around, you'll soon
discover all the details hidden in each picture.
When you have finished, put the torch
back in its pocket on the last page.

What goes on under the city?

In a city, you see buildings, streets and statues. There are a lot of things below the streets you can't see. To discover what is hidden down there, use your magic torch.

Below the buildings, parking lots!

There are too many cars in our cities
and not enough parking spaces.
More and more buildings now
have underground parking lots.

Below the pavements, pipes!

Often you see workmen digging up the streets. They are repairing water or gas pipes. Sometimes they are laying new electricity cables.

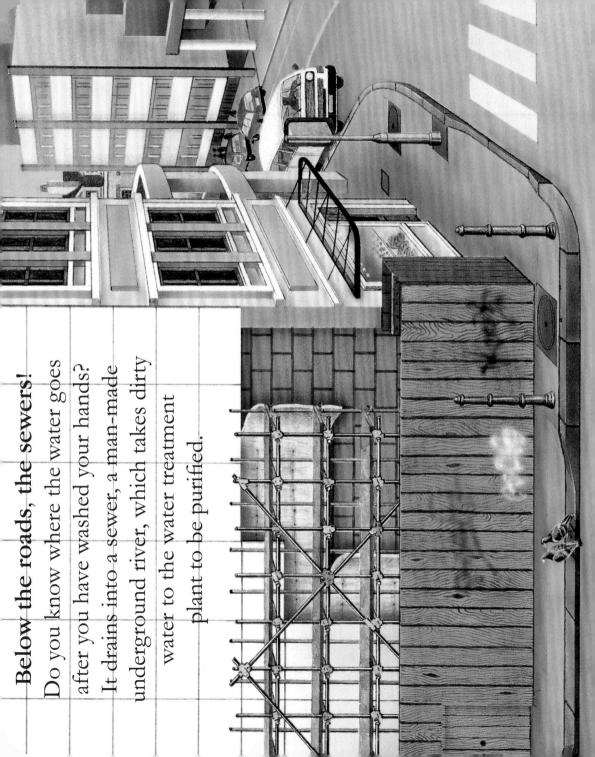

Below the roads, the sewers!

Do you know where the water goes
after you have washed your hands?
It drains into a sewer, a man-made
underground river, which takes dirty
water to the water treatment
plant to be purified.

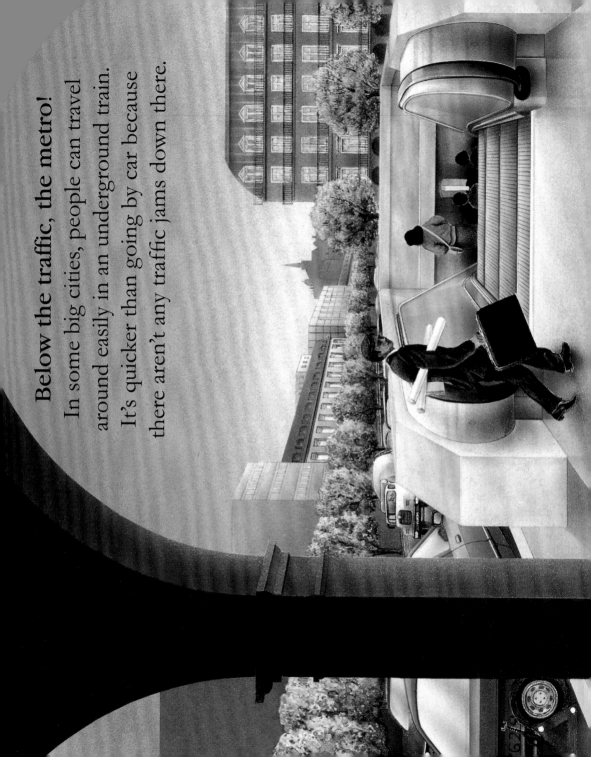

Below the traffic, the metro!

In some big cities, people can travel around easily in an underground train. It's quicker than going by car because there aren't any traffic jams down there.

Below the sea, a train!

Engineers built a very long tunnel under the sea to join Britain and France. Eurostar carries train passengers, and Eurotunnel takes cars and trucks on freight trains.

Under the square, the old city!

Sometimes, when builders are digging,
they find ancient remains of the city.
Archaeologists come to work on the site
and find out how the city used to be.

Sometimes a new building has an underground shopping centre.

The computer room, the staff lounge and the canteen of this big company building are all underground.

The drinking water for a city is tested several times each day in the water treatment plant.

Mushrooms are often grown in cities in huge underground cellars.

These details are from the dark pages of the book.

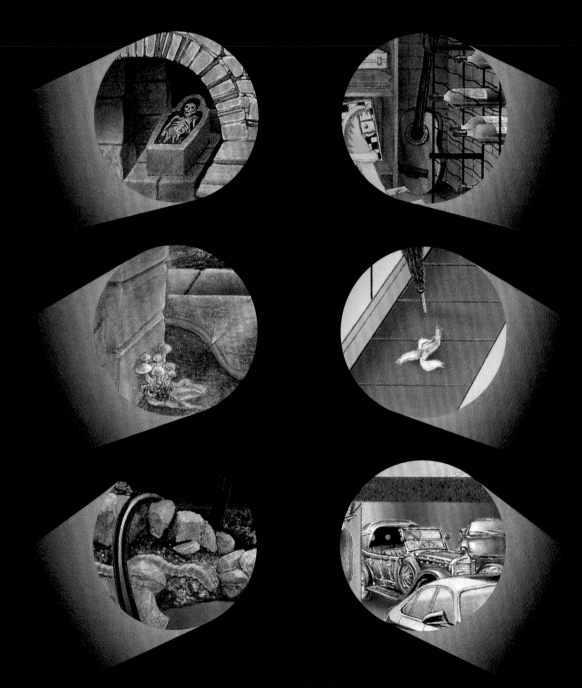

Can you find them using your magic torch?

MY FIRST DISCOVERY PAPERBACKS

Classics

Dinosaurs	Fruit	The Town
The Egg	Homes	Trains
Farm Animals	The Jungle	Trees
Firefighting	Planes	Vegetables
Flowers	The Seashore	Water

Torchlights

Animals Underground
Arcimboldo's Portraits
Insects
Inside the Body
Life below the City

Translated by Penelope Stanley-Baker
ISBN: 978-1-85103-763-6
© Éditions Gallimard Jeunesse, 1997.
English Text © Moonlight Publishing Ltd, 2022.
English audio rights Ⓟ Moonlight Publishing Ltd, 2022.
First published in the United Kingdom in 2022
by Moonlight Publishing Ltd,
2 Michael's Court, Hanney Road,
Southmoor, Oxfordshire, OX13 5HR
United Kingdom
Printed in China